EYEWITNESS TO HISTORY

HENRY FORD

in his own words

Gareth Stevens
PUBLISHING

By Ryan Nagelhout

Please visit our website, www.garethstevens.com. For a free color catalog of all our high-quality books, call toll free 1-800-542-2595 or fax 1-877-542-2596.

Library of Congress Cataloging-in-Publication Data

Nagelhout, Ryan.
Henry Ford in his own words / by Ryan Nagelhout.
p. cm. — (Eyewitness to history)
Includes index.
ISBN 978-1-4824-1279-6 (pbk.)
ISBN 978-1-4824-1218-5 (6-pack)
ISBN 978-1-4824-1480-6 (library binding)
1. Ford, Henry, — 1863-1947 — Juvenile literature. 2. Automobile industry and trade — United States — Biography — Juvenile literature. 3. Industrialists — United States — Biography — Juvenile literature. I. Nagelhout, Ryan. II. Title.
TL140.F6 N34 2015
338.7—d23

First Edition

Published in 2015 by
Gareth Stevens Publishing
111 East 14th Street, Suite 349
New York, NY 10003

Copyright © 2015 Gareth Stevens Publishing

Designer: Katelyn E. Reynolds
Editor: Therese Shea

Photo credits: Cover, p. 1 (Henry) courtesy of Library of Congress; cover, pp. 1 (background illustration), 8 Hulton Archive/Getty Images; cover, p. 1 (logo quill icon) Seamartini Graphics Media/Shutterstock.com; cover, p. 1 (logo stamp) YasnaTen/ Shutterstock.com; cover, p. 1 (color grunge frame) DmitryPrudnichenko/Shutterstock.com; cover, pp. 1–32 (paper background) Nella/Shutterstock.com; cover, pp. 1–32 (decorative elements) Ozerina Anna/Shutterstock.com; pp. 1–32 (wood texture) Reinhold Leitner/ Shutterstock.com; pp. 1–32 (open book background) Elena Schweitzer/Shutterstock.com; pp. 1–32 (bookmark) Robert Adrian Hillman/Shutterstock.com; pp. 4, 5 TimePix/Time Life Pictures/Getty Images; pp. 7, 9, 19 (both) from the Collections of The Henry Ford/Gift of Ford Motor Company; p. 11 Newsweek/Wikipedia.com; p. 12 (logo) Wikipedia.com; pp. 12–13 National Motor Museum/Heritage Images/Getty Images; p. 14 Mansell/Time Life Pictures/Getty Images; p. 15 SSPL/Getty Images; p. 16 Connormah/Henry Ford/Wikipedia.com; pp. 17 (ad), 22 Fotosearch/Getty Images; p. 17 (photo) Universal History Archive/Getty Images; pp. 20–21 Keystone-France/ Gamma-Keystone/Getty Images; p. 23 Dave Parker/Wikipedia.com; p. 24 Sekicho/ Wikipedia.com; p. 25 Amit Evron/Wikipedia.com; p. 27 MPI/Getty Images; p. 28 Danita Delimont/Gallo Images/Getty Images.

Printed in the United States of America

CPSIA compliance information: Batch #CS15GS: For further information contact Gareth Stevens, New York, New York at 1-800-542-2595.

CONTENTS

*Words in the glossary appear in **bold** type the first time they are used in the text.*

HUMBLE *Beginnings*

Henry Ford was born July 30, 1863, in Greenfield Township, Michigan. Ford's parents, William and Mary, owned a seven-room house on a successful farm near Detroit. Henry Ford's life could have easily been spent on his father's farm, but he soon established his own path.

Ford was a curious boy growing up. He loved to tinker with machines, which means he took them apart and repaired and adjusted them

Dearborn was settled in 1786 and became a city in 1929. The Ford Motor Company was a key business in its growth.

FORD MOTOR COMPANY

Henry Ford, 1893

In 1916, Ford was quoted in the *Chicago Tribune* as saying "*history is more or less bunk.*" The article got him in trouble, and Ford defended himself by explaining that the history many are taught doesn't focus on all people. Ford believed that history should be about the lives of ordinary people and everyday life, not kings and generals. Ford believed that his life's work should be dedicated to ordinary people and their lives, too.

just to learn how they worked. It would be his inventions and **innovations** that helped change the entire country, including his hometown. During his life, Ford would see Greenfield Township become part of Detroit and later Dearborn. He would build factories and museums there, all celebrating his life's work: the Ford Motor Company.

TINKERING

Ford loved to do experiments when he was young. He once tied the lid of a pot of water down and put the pot on an open fire. The pot exploded, burning Ford with scalding water, but he remained fascinated with the power of steam. He famously said, *"Thinking calls for facts; facts are found by digging; but he who has gathered this wealth is well equipped for life."* The early lessons Ford learned shaped his later life.

Ford loved to learn, but he only completed school up to the sixth grade. *"Any man can learn anything he will,"* Ford said, *"but no man can teach except to those who want to learn."* What Ford wanted to learn about was machines. He learned how to build steam engines and later how to operate full-size engines. His teachers were the men who ran them.

Ford also taught himself how to fix watches. After his mother died when he was 12, a heartbroken Ford said that, without his mother, his *"house was now a watch without a mainspring."* In 1879, he left his father's farm to be an **apprentice** at the Michigan Car Company, which made railroad cars in Detroit.

Understanding the complex designs of watches helped Ford learn more about how machines worked.

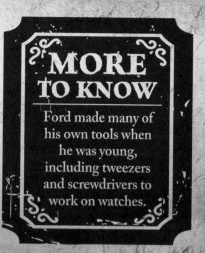

MORE TO KNOW

Ford made many of his own tools when he was young, including tweezers and screwdrivers to work on watches.

Henry Ford was just 16 when he left home for Detroit. He didn't make much money—about $2.50 a week—but he learned about machinery. He returned home in 1882 to operate and service steam-engine farm machinery. He also worked in factories and cut timber to sell.

MORE TO KNOW

Ford was responsible for keeping the power on in Detroit 24 hours a day.

In 1888, Ford married Clara Bryant. They moved to Detroit in 1891, where he took a job as an engineer for the Edison Electric **Illuminating** Company. Ford became the chief engineer in just 5 years, but in his spare time, he worked on a variety of other projects. *"It has been my observation that most people get ahead during the time that others waste,"* Ford said. He was spending his nights working on the next great American invention—the horseless carriage, which was an early name for the automobile.

Henry Ford is circled in this photo of Edison Electric Illuminating Company employees.

THE "GREAT BELIEVER"

Henry and Clara Bryant were married on April 11, 1888, in Clara's home. Henry's father gave the couple a farm where Henry built their "honeymoon cottage" using some of the lumber from the trees there. Ford later said that *the greatest day of my life was the day I married Mrs. Ford.*" He described his wife as the *"great believer,"* the one person who always supported his passions and goals as an inventor.

Henry and Clara Ford enjoyed many activities together, including traveling and dancing.

The QUADRICYCLE

BREAKING DOWN THE WALL

Ford and his friends put together the Quadricycle in a brick shed on his property. It was built on a steel frame, and its seat looked like a toolbox. When the vehicle was finally ready to test, Ford realized the door wasn't wide enough for the Quadricycle to get out! So, he took an axe and knocked down part of a brick wall to allow it to pass through.

In 1896, Ford and a group of friends produced their first **self-propelled** vehicle. Called the Quadricycle, it had a gas-powered engine and four wire wheels that looked like large bicycle wheels. It was steered with a **rudder**, somewhat like a boat. The Quadricycle was small, only had two forward speeds, and couldn't go in reverse—but it worked. Ford hopped in and drove it for a few blocks before it broke down.

"The only real mistake is the one from which we learn nothing," Ford later said. Despite issues with the vehicle, he was encouraged. Two years later, he had a second automobile. This time the design was simpler and more suited for production. Ford left Edison Electric and started finding investors for a new automobile company.

MORE TO KNOW

Thomas Edison encouraged Ford to build the gas-powered car when he first met him: *"Young man, that's the thing! You have it—the self-contained unit carrying its own fuel with it! Keep at it!"*

Ford's Quadricycle weighed 500 pounds (227 kg). He sold it, but later bought it back.

STOPS
and Starts

Henry Ford was finally in the business of making cars, but he didn't find success right away. His first group of investors for the Detroit Automobile Company grew tired of waiting for a product that satisfied Ford and closed the business after a year and a half. In 1901, Ford tried again with the Henry Ford Company. Less than a year after starting that company, Ford left it. Still, he remained hopeful about the future.

"*Failure is simply the opportunity to begin again this time more intelligently,*" Ford said. He spent the next year improving his designs and even racing his cars to draw interest in them. He convinced a man named James Couzens to work with him and gather investors. On June 16, 1903, the Ford Motor Company was founded.

Famous racer Barney Oldfield sits in the 999, while Henry Ford stands at right.

THE 999 AND THE ARROW

Ford started racing cars to generate interest and investors for his business. His first racing car, dubbed the "999," was driven by Barney Oldfield. In 1904, Ford drove his second race car, the Arrow, on the ice of Lake St. Clair. The Arrow went 91.37 miles (147.05 km) per hour, setting a world land speed record. Later in life, Ford said to Oldfield, "*You made me and I made you.*" Oldfield replied, "*Old 999 made both of us.*"

MODEL *Cars*

THE BIG TWELVE

The Ford Motor Company had 12 original investors when it was started in 1903. Ford himself had spent more than $25,000 of his own money on the company and didn't have any more to pitch in. Some investors, like Charles J. Woodall, gave $1,000 and made a few thousand dollars on their investment in a few years. James Couzens, who later became the company's business manager, invested $2,500. He made more than $29 million by 1919!

With a factory ready and a design finalized, the Ford Motor Company produced its Model A just a few months after the company formed. Ford's goal was to make *"a motor car for the great multitude,"* which means he wanted to build cars almost

A family proudly sits in their Ford Model A.

everyone could afford to buy. He didn't want cars to just be for the very rich. Ford worked hard to simplify the design and parts to save money. The Model A cost $850 dollars, which is about $23,000 in today's money.

Ford's next car, the Model N, cost $600 and was first sold in 1906. Simple but affordable, the Model N was another hit. By the next year, it was the best-selling car in the United States.

MORE TO KNOW

The Model N's standard features included sidelights, a taillight, and a horn. Anything else cost extra.

Model N

The MODEL T

The Ford company began building its most famous car on October 1, 1908. Henry Ford was still focused on simplicity and affordability. Every part on each car was the

MORE TO KNOW

Ford sold 1 million Model Ts in just 7 years.

same. *"Any customer can have a car painted any color he wants,"* Ford said, *"so long as it is black."*

The Model T cost $850. In 1909, Ford sold 10,600 Model T cars. They were reliable and affordable; Ford couldn't make enough of them. So the company moved to a large new plant in 1910. Ford borrowed ideas from other companies to better organize the way each car was made. In 1913, the Ford Motor Company moving assembly line helped make Model Ts cheaper to put together. Instead of increasing his profit, though, Ford lowered the cost of each car.

Henry Ford's actual signature:

Henry Ford

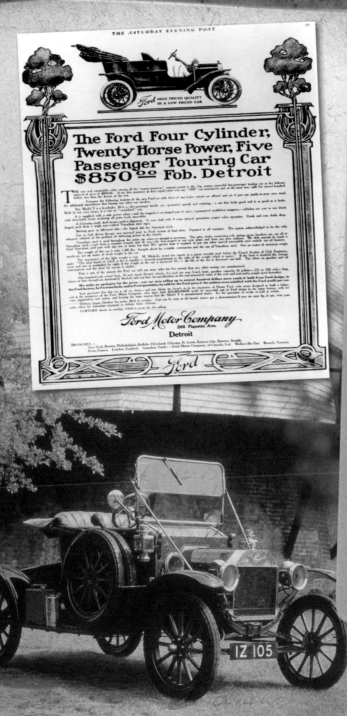

The moving assembly line allowed the Ford company to build its Model Ts very quickly. About 3,000 parts went into each Model T.

THE ASSEMBLY LINE

On the moving assembly line, each employee did a single job to make each car. As cars moved down the line, the worker would put one part on each car. There were 84 different steps to making a Model T. Each group of workers completed a step as the car was pulled down the assembly line on a rope. Cars were made much faster this way. Production time went down from about 12 hours for each car to about 90 minutes.

The $5 DAY

The assembly line let Ford build cars much faster, but many workers grew tired of doing the same task over and over again and soon quit. Ford had to hire 53,000 people a year to keep enough workers in his factories. He thought that paying workers more would keep them happy.

At a 1914 Ford management meeting, the businessmen worked out how much the company could afford to raise daily wages until *"finally the wage of $2.34 stood at $4.75."* Another man said jokingly that if they were going to be *"fools,"* they should be *"first-class fools"* and make it even larger—$5. *"All right, let's make it $5,"* Ford said. Ford wanted to share company profits with his workers so they stayed loyal. He also shortened the workday from 9 hours to 8 hours.

PEACE SHIP

Ford was a pacifist, or someone who doesn't believe in war. In 1915, he sailed to Europe on the ship *Oskar II* to seek an end to World War I, which was fought 1914 to 1918. At the time, the United States wasn't fighting in the war. The voyage was a failure. *"I wanted to see peace,"* Ford said about the journey. *"I at least tried to bring it about. Most men did not even try."*

In 1914, the company announced it would more than double the normal pay for an 8-hour workday. It made headlines across the country.

'GOLD RUSH' IS STARTED BY FORD'S $5 OFFER

Thousands of Men Seek Employment in Detroit Factory.

Will Distribute $10,000,000 in Semi-Monthly Bonuses.

No Employe to Receive Less Than Five Dollars a Day.

(TIMES-STAR SPECIAL DISPATCH.)
DETROIT, Mich., January 7.—
Henry Ford in an interview to-

RUNAWAY
Success

Ford produced the Model T for 19 years. Its cost continued to drop as sales increased. In 1922, a two-seat Model T started at $269. By 1925, Ford was making 2 million Model Ts a year. After nearly two decades of sales, however, customers wanted a new kind of car. Ford wanted to keep making the Model T but realized the nation's needs were changing.

"*The Model T car was a pioneer,*" Ford wrote in 1927. "*There was no **conscious** public need of motor cars when we first made it. There were few good roads. This car blazed the way*

MORE TO KNOW

Ford made 55 percent of the auto industry's cars in 1921.

Ford began selling a new car, again called the Model A, in 1927. Edsel Ford is pictured to the right of his father.

for the motor industry & started the movement for good roads everywhere. . . . But conditions in this country have so greatly changed that further refinement in motor car construction is now desirable."

TAKING CONTROL

In 1919, Ford bought out the remaining investors in the Ford Motor Company. Many of the men became millionaires. James Couzens' sister made $262,036.67 for $100 he borrowed from her for his investment. Henry Ford now owned the largest car company in the world. He made his 26-year-old son, Edsel, president of the company, but he still controlled everything the Ford company did. *"Businesses that grow by development and improvement do not die,"* Ford said in 1923.

On the
HOMESTEAD

THE VAGABONDS

From 1913 to 1924, Ford and a few friends took an annual 2-week camping trip. Many of those trips included three of his close friends: inventor Thomas Edison, businessman Harvey Firestone, and poet John Burroughs. The four men called themselves the Vagabonds and visited many spots throughout the country, including the Adirondack and the Great Smoky Mountains. Each year the trips grew larger, with photographers on hand to take pictures. Even a few presidents joined them.

As the Ford Motor Company grew, the Ford family grew out of their home. Ford bought 1,300 acres (527 ha) of land in Dearborn about 2 miles (3 km) from his father's farm. He started building a 56-room limestone house he called Fair Lane. In 1915, the Fords moved into Fair Lane, which included several cottages, gardens, and a library of 4,000 books.

(from left to right) Thomas Edison, John Burroughs, Henry Ford, and Harvey Firestone

Some of Henry and Clara's happiest times were spent relaxing or entertaining at Fair Lane. While the house was filled with beautiful things, it was also comfortable. Clara said, *"Our house is not just a showplace but a place to enjoy and live."* Others enjoyed it, too. Thomas Edison had his own special rooms at Fair Lane.

Fair Lane was made a National Historic Landmark in 1966.

MORE TO KNOW

Despite his success building cars, Henry Ford wasn't the best driver. He *"didn't concern himself with such things as stop signs and stop lights,"* according to one of his employees at Fair Lane.

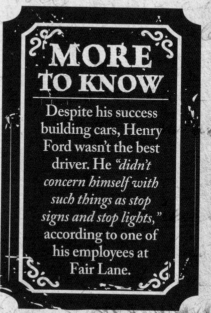

INNOVATION
and Failure

As with all inventors, Ford's ideas were hit and miss. He built some airplanes; his most famous had three engines in it. He opened the Ford Airport in Dearborn in 1925, too. In all, he spent $11 million on aviation before quitting in 1932. Though he never made a profit, he believed aviation had a great future. He even predicted, *"Mark my word: A combination airplane and motor car is coming."* That vehicle still hasn't been invented, though.

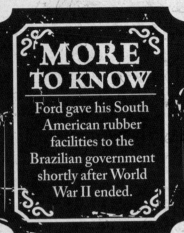

MORE TO KNOW

Ford gave his South American rubber facilities to the Brazilian government shortly after World War II ended.

Ford said, "We are not going to South America to make money but to help develop that wonderful and fertile land . . . We'll train the Brazilians and they'll work as well as any others."

KINGSFORD CHARCOAL

Ford started another successful company while making cars in Michigan. At that time, Model Ts were made of wood. In the 1920s, Ford discovered that scrap wood from his factories could be used to make charcoal briquettes, or blocks of carbon burned as fuel for cooking. Ford soon started the Kingsford Charcoal company. He named the company after his wife's brother, E. G. Kingsford, who helped him buy the land to build the factory on.

In the meantime, Ford Motor Company continued to grow, introducing the light and affordable **V8** engine in 1932. Ford also tried to build his own rubber facilities in Brazil between 1928 and 1945. Communities called Fordlandia and Belterra were established. They had many problems with both the rubber trees and the workers. There were even riots over conditions.

THE GOOD
and the Bad

Ford became a **controversial** figure in his later years. He allowed **anti-Semitic** articles to be published in a newspaper he owned, *The Dearborn Independent*. He later publicly apologized. He also battled **labor unions** that demanded more pay and better working conditions in his factories.

However, the Ford Motor Company proudly hired immigrants and disabled war veterans. They employed African Americans decades before other companies were forced to during the **civil rights movement** of the 1950s and 1960s.

A SENATE RUN

In 1918, President Woodrow Wilson convinced Ford to run for a seat in the US Senate. Ford ran as a Democrat but didn't want to spend any money on an election campaign. *"If they want to elect me let them do so,"* Ford wrote President Wilson, *"But I won't make a penny's investment."* Ford followed through on his vow not to spend any money on his campaign and lost by only 4,500 votes to Republican Truman Newberry.

Ford had a very long battle with the United Auto Workers (UAW) union. Seconds after this photograph was taken in 1937, the Ford guards on the left attacked the UAW men on the right.

Henry Ford also stood by his belief that his company should help its workers make money and stay happy. *"From the start I had my own ideas about how the business should run,"* Ford said in 1941. *"I wanted it to benefit everybody who contributed to its success—stockholders, labor and the American public."*

MORE TO KNOW

On May 26, 1937, labor union organizers clashed violently with Ford Motor Company security guards at a plant in Dearborn, Michigan. It was called the Battle of the Overpass.

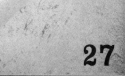

HISTORY
Worth Observing

Henry Ford died at Fair Lane on April 7, 1947, at the age of 83. Though the automaker once called history *"bunk,"* he spent much of his later years trying to preserve the history of the American people. *"That's the only history that is worth observing,"* he said in 1919. *"We're going to build a museum that's going to show industrial history, and it won't be bunk!"*

The Edison Institute, now called the Henry Ford, was opened in Dearborn in 1929. Today it has libraries, a museum, and a village that features re-creations of places and objects from the past, including the Model T and many other innovations produced by Henry Ford and the Ford Motor Company.

MORE TO KNOW

Ford wanted his Edison Institute to *"reproduce the life of the country in its every age."*

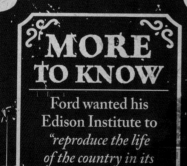

the Henry Ford

TIMELINE
THE LIFE OF HENRY FORD

Born in Greenfield Township, Michigan, on July 30 — **1863**

1879 — Leaves family farm for Detroit to apprentice in machine shops

Marries Clara Bryant on April 11 — **1888**

1891 — Hired as engineer at Edison Electric Illuminating Company

Produces his first automobile, the Quadricycle — **1896**

1903 — Starts Ford Motor Company; builds Model A

Begins building Model T — **1908**

1913 — Installs first moving assembly line

Sets sail on *Oskar II* to speak out against World War I — **1915**

1918 — Loses bid for US Senate

Buys out other investors; makes son Edsel company president — **1919**

1924 — 10-millionth Model T is produced

Opens Edison Institute — **1929**

1932 — Introduces V8 car

Dies on April 7 at Fair Lane — **1947**

EDUCATIONAL ESTATE

After the Fords died, the company let the University of Michigan build part of its campus on the Fair Lane property. The house is now a museum, but other buildings are used by the school. Though he didn't attend school for long, Ford thought people should always be educating themselves. *"All life is experience,"* he said, *"and one level is exchanged for another only when its lesson is learned."*

29

GLOSSARY

anti-Semitic: hating Jewish people or treating them badly

apprentice: someone who learns a trade by working with a skilled person of that trade

bunk: nonsense

civil rights movement: a time period in US history starting in the 1950s in which African Americans fought for equal civil rights, or the freedoms granted to us by law

conscious: aware, mindful

controversial: causing strong disagreement or disapproval

illuminate: to light up

innovation: a new invention, or a new way of doing things

labor union: a group of workers who join together to argue for better benefits

mainspring: the most important spring in a mechanical device

rudder: the part on a boat or plane that helps steer

self-propelled: the ability to move itself without aid

V8: an engine with two banks of four cylinders arranged in a V shape

FOR MORE
Information

Books

Abrams, Dennis. *The Invention of the Moving Assembly Line: A Revolution in Manufacturing*. New York, NY: Chelsea House, 2011.

Gregory, Josh. *Henry Ford: Father of the Auto Industry*. New York, NY: Children's Press, 2014.

Roberts, Steven. *Henry Ford*. New York, NY: PowerKids Press, 2013.

Websites

The Henry Ford Estate
www.henryfordestate.org
This site has information about visiting Fair Lane on the Henry Ford Estate.

Henry Ford Quotations
thehenryford.org/research/henryFordQuotes.aspx
This page has many quotes from throughout Ford's life.

The Life of Henry Ford
hfmgv.org/exhibits/hf/
Learn more about Henry Ford and view many photos of the inventor.

INDEX